T0196235

WHAT
SHOULD WE
BELIEVE?

CREATION OR EVOLUTION

Also by Thomas Eristhee:

The Church Revealed
Now You Are Saved, What Next?
Satan Exposed

WHAT SHOULD WE BELIEVE?

CREATION OR EVOLUTION

Thomas Eristhee

iUniverse, Inc.
New York   Bloomington

What Should we Believe?
Creation or Evolution

iUniverse books may be ordered through booksellers or by contacting:

iUniverse
1663 Liberty Drive
Bloomington, IN 47403
www.iuniverse.com
1-800-Authors (1-800-288-4677)

Because of the dynamic nature of the Internet, any Web addresses or links contained in this book may have changed since publication and may no longer be valid. The views expressed in this work are solely those of the author and do not necessarily reflect the views of the publisher, and the publisher hereby disclaims any responsibility for them.

ISBN: 978-1-4401-4237-6 (pbk)
ISBN: 978-1-4401-4236-9 (ebk)

Printed in the United States of America

iUniverse rev. date: 6/03/2009

TABLE OF CONTENTS

Book 1

Book 2

BOOK 1

PROOF THAT GOD EXISTS

INTRODUCTION

It is very important to the Christian that we have evidence that God exists; not just personal evidence but evidence that is apparent to all, including unbelievers. Once the evidence of God's existence becomes obvious, then the unbelievers would be able to look at the facts and might turn to God the Creator, and worship Him in Spirit and in truth. We can only believe God through faith, but there are a number of things that can help build up our faith.

Many have been saved because they witnessed a miracle right before their very eyes; yet others have been saved through personal revelation, where God, in some special way, revealed Himself to them. There are those who have looked at nature and say, 'there is somebody greater than man and I would like to know Him.' Others have said, 'God if you are there send me some direction' and He has done that.

Of course there are great testimonies of people who got saved just by reading the Bible. We do not need to believe that God exists to make God exist. Whether we believe it or not God exists. However these evidences are for our help, to build up our faith in God. How would we preach Christ if we did not have evidence? Surely it would be much more difficult than it is now.

I am so glad that we have evidence, and I am part of that evidence because He has changed my life completely, in a way nobody else could have. And those who knew me before I was saved and who know me now, know that God has done a work in my life; they have the evidence as to how God can change a sinner into a saint. All true Christians are evidences of the existence of God.

CONSCIENCE GIVES PROOF OF THE EXISTENCE OF GOD

Karl Rahner, in defining conscience said, "While it is used in many senses both in popular and scientific language, it donates, in its specifically moral usage, a series of related phenomena of the soul, the kernel of which is an impressive basic experience reaching deep into personal consciousness."[1]

From within ourselves we know that there are things that are right and things that are wrong. How or why do we think that way? I say God has put His law in our conscience; right and wrong; good and evil, God or the devil. We cannot run away from it.

If there is evil (and we know there is), then there is good. If the devil is the leader of evil, then God is the leader of that which is good.

"Man's failure to acknowledge God as Lord of creation is understandable but inexcusable," says Karl Rahner.[2] Because his conscience continue to bear him record, man can run away from human

---

[1]   Encyclopedia of Theology. Karl Rahner; p. 283
[2]   Encyclopedia of Theology. Karl Rahner; p. 283

reasoning and logical arguments, but he cannot run away from his own conscience.

Romans 1:19-21 says: "Because that which may be known of God is manifest in them; for God hath shewed it unto them. For the invisible things of Him from the creation of the world are clearly seen, being understood by the things that are made, even His eternal power and godhead; so that they are without excuse: Because that, when they knew God, they glorified Him not as God, neither were thankful; but became vain in their imaginations, and their foolish heart was darkened."

They knew God because God spoke to their conscience; God made Himself known, not a preacher. So man is without excuse, because God Himself spoke to man. At times we talk about the man who never had someone to talk to him about God, and we ask the question, "What would happen to that person?" My answer is, God has a way of talking to people that we may never know; but we can be sure of one thing, He speaks to people through their consciences.

John Calvin states, "There has been no society since the beginning of the world, no city, no home, that could exist without religion. This fact in itself points to a sense of divinity inscribed in the hearts of all people."[3]

People know that there is a God; this is why there is religion in every nation and tongue. They may not be worshipping the true God, but they know there is a God; conscience is bearing them witness. There is an attempt by some to get rid of God, but man cannot, because you cannot get rid of conscience. The law of God is not just in the Bible; it has been written in man's conscience.

That is why we cannot get rid of right and wrong; conscience will let us know that we have done wrong. I am not saying that conscience is the only law; neither am I saying that if conscience does not condemn us we are free – NO! All I am saying is that conscience is one of the tools that God is using to let us know that He exists and we cannot run away from it.

We read from John R. Willis, "The knowledge

---

[3] The Christian of Theology Reader. Alister E. Mc. Grath; p. 57

of Himself God placed within man from the beginning. But this knowledge they invested stocks and stones with, and so dealt unrighteously to the truth, as far at least as they might."[4]

The knowledge of God is so much in man that we set up systems in our nations as to how we should govern ourselves. We put laws and people in place to see to it that our laws are observed. And according to our laws, there is punishment for those who disobey the law.

There is something embedded in us by God about good and evil. Many times we find that some people escape from the punishment they justly deserve based on the crime they committed. And they escape for many reasons; at times they are able to afford good lawyers; maybe they were popular and the judge had mercy on them because of association, or maybe they ran away and were never found.

Yet somehow we believe that they will pay for it; we believe that justice will be served from some spiritual realm. And it seems as if we see it happening to them in this life; and of course we who are

---

[4]   The Teachings of The Church Fathers. John R. Willis S J; p. 137

saved know that if they do not repent they will have a miserable future. We believe there is one, who is greater than our justice system, and man can run but they cannot hide from Him.

C.S. Lewis, talking about the law in man's heart, puts it this way, "Quarrelling means trying show that the other man's in the wrong, and there would be no sense in trying to do that unless you and he had some sort of agreement as to what is right and wrong."[5]

We are forced to believe in God by our own behavior; we know that there is an inner reality, a rule that we must adhere to. When we don't, we know we are guilty. It is God speaking to us through conscience.

---

[5] The Case For Christianity. C. S. Lewis; p.4

GOD'S REVELATION THROUGH MIRACLES

Wayne Grudem, in his book Systematic Theology, defines miracles as, "A direct intervention of God in the world."[6] Another definition in that same book is, "God acting contrary to the laws of nature."[7]

These definitions, and there are many more like them in other books, see God as the source of miracles. He intervenes the laws of nature; He acts contrary to the laws of nature. So if these definitions are true about miracles, then from the time a miracle takes place, we know that God was at work.

At times words like, signs, wonders, mighty works, are used instead of the word, 'miracle'. When we talk about wonders, first of all, it makes us wonder, how something happened, because as far as we all knew there was no means of causing it to happen. They are called mighty works because they could not have been done by ordinary man or by natural ability.

---

[6] Systematic Theology. Wayne Grudem; p. 355
[7] Systematic Theology. Wayne Grudem; p. 355

Nicodemus came to Jesus because he realized that the miracles that Jesus was doing could only have been done if God was with Jesus. This is what he said in **John 3:2, "The same came to Jesus by night, and said unto Him, Rabbi, we know that thou art a teacher sent from God: because no man can do these miracles that thou doest, except God be with him."**

In the book of **John 9:3** we have the story of a man that was born blind. The disciples asked Him what the cause of that blindness was; this is the response that Jesus gave: **"...Neither hath this man sinned, nor his parents: but that the works of God should be made manifest in him."** So miracles are seen as the work of God by Jesus.

There is a set way that things function; a normal way or natural way. For example, if you throw a stone up, you expect it to come down; because of the natural law of gravity, it cannot stay in the air. We cannot walk on water; if it is fire then it is hot, it would burn. So if a man is truly walking on water, it is a miracle. If a man is truly dead and is raised after three days – this is a miracle.

Now, according to natural laws and science, this is not supposed to have been done, but God did it to prove to humanity that there is one greater than water and one who can step in and do as He pleases, when He pleases, what no other man or woman can do.

Stephen Charnock says, "That which cannot be the result of a natural cause, must be the result of something supernatural; what is beyond the reach of nature is the effect of a power superior to nature, for it is quite against the order of nature and is the elevation of something to such a pitch, which all nature could not advance it to."[8]

Man is aware of the fact that there are things happening, and things that have happened, that cannot be the result of any other than God's intervention. Now I know everybody knows about miracles, many have experienced one or had some close friends who did; or at least have heard of one and was convinced that it was genuine.

To whom or to what do they ascribe these miracles? The miracles that took place in the Bible were

---

[8]   The Existence and Attributes of God. Stephen Charnock; p. 76

not just witnessed by Christians alone; many of the heathen saw and some believed, because of the miracles. For instance, let us look at the crucifixion and the miracles that took place after it.

Matthew 27: 50-54 says, "Jesus, when he had cried again with a loud voice, yielded up the ghost. And, behold, the veil of the temple was rent in twain from the top to the bottom; and the earth did quake, and the rocks rent; and the graves were opened; and many bodies of the saints which slept arose, and came out of the graves after his resurrection, and went into the holy city, and appeared to many. Now when the centurion and they that were with him, watching Jesus, saw the earthquake, and those things that were done, they feared greatly, saying, Truly this was the Son of God."

So even the unbelievers understood by miracles that Jesus was the Son of God; basically He was who He said He was. With the raising of Lazarus from the dead, the Bible says in **John 11:45, "Then many of the Jews which came to Mary, and had seen the things that Jesus did, believed on Him."** Now after the miracles of raising Lazarus from the dead, the enemies of Jesus realized that through these miracles people were putting their trust in God; they tried to kill Jesus and also Lazarus; they tried to kill both the one who performed the miracle and the evidence of the miracle – Lazarus.

They wanted to stop the people from believing in Jesus but as long as the miracle stands, the people will believe. So the miracles were proof that God was working through Jesus. Now let us hear what the enemy says:

"If we let him thus alone, all men will believe on him: and the Romans shall come and take away both our place and nation." John 11:48. Miracles are there to prove that there is a God, and that people will believe on Him.

Paul Davies says, "The scientific quest is a journey into the unknown; each advance brings new and unexpected discoveries and challenges our minds with unusual and sometimes difficult concepts."[9]

There are some miracles that there are no explanations for, but they are examples of the divine move of God; He intervened in human life.

---

9   The Mind Of God. Paul Davies; p. 21

EVIDENCE FROM CREATION

Man has power to make many things such as houses, automobiles etc. But whatever a man creates or makes has a short life time; by that I mean they do not last forever. But we see a world around us since the beginning of time, which we don't know a quarter about, in spite of the fact that we have taken so much time to study it. So we must know that there is a greater person than ourselves; a master creator who doeth all things right, who created the heavens and the earth. These are physical evidences that there is a God. Not only is he able to create but He is able to hold creation together by His power. He changes times and seasons, He brings day and night, heat and cold.

From the beginning God put structure in place that man can know Him if they look at the creation of the world. If our eyes can adore this material universe, should not our hearts desire to see and know the Maker of all we behold? Because we certainly know that the Maker is greater than the creation, and if the creation is so beautiful then the Maker should be the most awesome thing to behold!

Instead of trying to deny that which is so obvious, what we should be trying or seeking after is to know the true God, the Creator of all that is in heaven and earth, of things we can see and things we cannot see, for surely there must be a creator.

St. Methodius said, "I began to praise the Creator, as I saw the earth fixed, and living creatures in such variety; and the blossoms of plants with their many hues, but my mind did not rest upon these things alone, but thereupon I began to inquire whence these have their origin. Whether from some source eternally co-existent with God, or from God Himself alone; none co-existent with Him, for that He has made nothing out of that which has no existence appeared to me, the right view to take."[10]

The proof of the existence of God through creation is one of the greatest proofs that we have; because you see it everyday, the proof is all around us. As a matter of fact, we are part of that process because we were created by someone greater than us.

---

[10]   The Teachings Of The Church Fathers. John R. Willis; p.135

He puts the system in place that life would continue through this mechanism, of which **Genesis 1:28 says: "And God blessed them, and said unto them, Be fruitful, and multiply, and replenish the earth, and subdue it: and have dominion over the fish of the sea, and over the fowl of the air, and over every living thing that moveth upon the earth."**

Now let us hear what the great apostle Paul says about knowing God through creation, in **Romans 1:20, "For the invisible things of him from the creation of the world are clearly seen, being understood by the things that are made, even his eternal power and Godhead, so that they are without excuse…"**

Because there has been revelation, man is without excuse. The revelation is public, all can see nature – revealing God; this revelation is general, everybody can know through creation. Not just the rich or only the poor, or based on one's location; no matter where in the world you are, you can see the power of God through His creation.

This creation did not die after our grandparents. It is continuous, all generations come and they see the evidence of the great God through creation. This evidence will be there as long as men are on the face of the earth. So Paul says that man is without excuse, both saved and unsaved, because they have the same evidence. The Jews as well as the Gentiles, all have creation as proof that God exists.

The creation of the universe is to bring praise to the creator. **Psalm 145:10-13 says: "All thy works shall praise thee, O LORD, and thy saints shall bless thee. They shall speak of the glory of thy kingdom, and talk of thy power; To make known to the sons of men his mighty acts, and the glorious majesty of his kingdom. Thy kingdom is an everlasting kingdom, and thy dominion endureth throughout all generations."**

This scripture says that creation shall speak of the glory of God's kingdom. So He is using creation to talk to His created about Himself.

In **Psalm 19:1-2** we read again, **"The heavens declare the glory of God; and the firmament sheweth his handywork. Day unto day uttereth speech, and night unto night sheweth knowledge."**

So from the school of creation or nature, man

should understand that there is a God and that he should be praised.

BIBLICAL EVIDENCE

From the first verse of the first book of the Bible great questions as to who created the universe was answered. Now it is left to us as to whom we will believe. Will we believe the Bible or some man? Now the following verse of scripture is probably the most important on the subject so let us read it.

"In the beginning God created the heaven and the earth." Genesis 1:1

So it plainly states who created and when; in the beginning, God created. No matter how long ago it was, God was the one who created it and that was in the beginning.

It is clear that everything begins with God based on scripture. Now if we believe scripture, then we believe in the existence of God because the Bible talks plainly about His existence. The Bible is not just words about God; it is the Word of God!

In **2 Timothy 3:16** we read, **"All scripture is given by inspiration of God, and is profitable for doctrine, for reproof, for correction, for instruction in righteousness."**

God used holy men to write what He wanted

them to write. This is how it is put in **2 Peter 1:21, "For the prophecy came not in old time by the will of man: but holy men of God spake as they were moved by the Holy Ghost."**

So they wrote down what God revealed to them. It has been there for thousands of years; the New Testament for about two thousand years and the Old Testament much more than that. I don't know of any book that has been around for so long, always in print, always selling well – it remains the same from beginning up to now.

I believe this is just a little to show that it is the book from God to us. The Bible is the most popular book in the world; therefore, everyone should read it so they can know what makes it so popular. Many people read all kinds of books about God, but they don't read the Book of God. If the Bible is God's book, and we want to know about God, then we should read it!

Day after day we are seeing scriptures being fulfilled before our eyes. Jesus said in **Matthew 5:18, "For verily I say unto you, Till heaven and earth**

pass, one jot or one tittle shall in no wise pass from the law, till all be fulfilled."

After Jesus had fasted forty days and forty nights, when He returned to the temple the Bible says in **Luke 4:17-19, "And there was delivered unto him the book of the prophet Esaias. And when he had opened the book, he found the place where it was written, The Spirit of the Lord is upon me, because he hath anointed me to preach the gospel to the poor; he hath sent me to heal the brokenhearted, to preach deliverance to the captives, and recovering of sight to the blind, to set at liberty them that are bruised, To preach the acceptable year of the Lord."**

Now let us see what verse 21 says: **"And he began to say unto them, This day is this scripture fulfilled in your ears."**

This scripture in Luke is a cross-reference to what Isaiah prophesied in **Isaiah 61:1-2** concerning Jesus. This was prophesied about eight hundred years before Christ was born. Now it is fulfilled; this has to be the Word of God.

How do we know that a prophecy is false? If it is not fulfilled. There are so many prophesies in the Old Testament, some over a thousand years before Jesus' birth, describing exactly how and where his birth would happen, and it came to pass exactly as they predicted. There are so many prophesies about His birth, death, burial and resurrection; all are fulfilled as prophesied.

The birth of Jesus Christ has its mark upon history even up to this time, when it comes to our calendar. This is what Paul E. Little had to say about it: "This child's life was destined to change the course of history. Two thousand years ago, His coming rocked the world. It changed its calendar, tailored its moves; the atheist in America dates his checks with a year dating approximately from Jesus' birth. The rulers of countries, both East and West, regardless of their religions, use His approximate birth year. Un-thinkingly, we declare His birth on letters, legal documents and date books. On the day we set aside to remember His birth..."[11]

Yes! We cannot deny this evidence. In the book

---

[11]   Know Why You Believe. Paul E. Little; p.38

of **2 Timothy 3:1** we read, **"This we know also, that in the last days perilous times shall come."** We are seeing it fulfilled before our very eyes; all that the Bible said would happen in the last days, is happening this very moment. The Bible is evidence that God exists.

GOD REVEALS HIMSELF

He has revealed Himself in history; bringing floods in the days of Noah was one of the ways God revealed Himself. He spoke to Noah before He did it and gave man time to repent of their evil – but they refused. So He sent a flood that destroyed man. The story about the flood is the story of a Holy God who hates unholiness. He proved this by destroying those who refused to turn away from wickedness, in spite of His warning to them.

Now, if we believe in Jesus' teaching, He made mention of the flood. He said in **Matthew 24:37-39, "But as the days of Noah were, so shall also the coming of the Son of man be. For as in the days that were before the flood they were eating and drinking, marrying and giving in marriage, until the day that Noah entered into the ark, And knew not until the flood came, and took them all away; so shall also the coming of the Son of man be."** The record of the flood is not just a biblical story.

Davis A. Young says, "Near Eastern archeological explorations during the past two centuries have shown that several versions of a deluge tradition were widely circulated throughout Mesopotamia and other parts of the Near East."[12]

And there is much more evidence from the non-Christian world about the flood. But this is what a man who does not understand God says, "Like most rulers who are soft on crime and unhappy with the results, God overreacted and swung the pendulum in the opposite direction."[13]

So he is accusing God of being as the weak rulers who are so soft on crime, that when they cannot control things, they revolt and commit massacres. He is implying that God had to kill men, women and children; to him many of them were innocent, and it was God who did not correct them from the beginning.

He continued his folly by saying, "In the early days of mankind, God too saw 'evil doing'. His response was to be 'sorry' that He had made human

---

[12] The Biblical Flood. Davis A. Young; p.5
[13] The Genesis of Justice. Alan M. Dershowitz; p. 62

beings; in the world of our translation and to kill everyone in the world except for one family, that of the righteous Noah."[14]

Man knows the truth but they will try to ridicule the truth; they will try to twist it or destroy it if possible, instead of doing that which is right that they may be spared when their day comes. God has spoken and man has heard, but just refuses to believe and practice the truth, because they love darkness rather than light.

Apart from the water and the evidence left, we understand that some claim that the ark that was used is still here after all these thousands of years. If this is true, would not this be the greatest evidence that God exists? Think about it – wood for about four thousand years, preserved somewhere only because divine eyes are upon it. Well, there are many who claim that the ark is still where it first landed after the flood.

Davis A. Young says, "Theophilus claimed that the remains are to this day to be seen in the Arabian mountains, he may have had in mind the Araba

---

[14]   The Genesis of Justice. Alan M. Dershowitz

Deserta, a piece of land that extends to the upper limits of the Mesopotamian Plain. If so, he would likely have been referring to Mount Qardu in the Gordyaean Hills north of Mesopotamia. Other writers explicitly located the ark in the Gordyaean Hills."[15]

Man knows that there is a God, and the Word of God gives evidence that God did something in history. Just because we know that the Word of God is true, we will search to see where we can find what the Word recorded happened, just because human beings know that the Bible is reliable.

[15] The Biblical Flood. Davis A. Young; p.20

UNIVERSABILITY OF BELIEF IN THE EXISTENCE OF GOD

Man everywhere believes in the existence of a supreme being or beings, who they worship in some form or refer to as the one who controls the universe. Now some may say not every one believes in God, but every nation I know believes in some kind of god, maybe not the true God; they probably establish their own god. But they believe in a god or some controller.

William Evans quoted an atheist who was talking to his friend about his belief or disbelief in God: "I have rid myself of the idea of a Supreme Being, and I thank God for it."[16] We may not be worshipping God, but we know He is there and we cannot get away from it, because there are people all around us worshipping Him; or at least a god.

Even when we were very small we began to ask questions like, 'Who created the world, who created the sea the sky?' and so on. We recognized that we

---

[16]   The Great doctrines Of The Bible. William Evans; p.15

grew up seeking for the right answers. But from what is around us, we are challenged to find out who is the master of it all; and the way the universe is so well organized tells us it is created by an intelligent designer, one who is full of power and might.

So as we began to grow in knowledge, we began to seek who is in charge of the world around us. It is just natural to ask who created the world in which we live.

Will Evans says, "That it could not come into being of itself seems obvious, not more than nails, brick, mortar, wood, paints, colors, form into a house or building of themselves; not more than the type composing a book came into order of itself."[17]

We build our houses; God who built the universe has given us power to build just as He builds, only in a different magnitude. We need material and hard labour; He does not. He creates out of nothing. The world was created by an intelligent designer and we came from Him. Therefore we have tremendous ability as the only one of His creation that He put

---

[17]   The Great doctrines Of The Bible. William Evans; p.16

His image in and baked with His own hands and He breathed His Spirit into our nostrils. That made us special and gave us charge over His creation down here on earth.

BOOK 2

CREATION OR EVOLUTION

INTRODUCTION

One may ask, "Why should we concern ourselves with the study of the universe as Christians? Are we not going too far? Shouldn't we be more concerned about the study of the Word of God? People want to hear what the Word says!"

God has spoken as to the creation of the universe, and I believe that if we do not have it right from there, probably we have it all wrong. The foundation must be prepared or else the building will collapse, whether it is a physical building or the building of the Christian faith.

The creation of the universe is one of the first things mentioned in the Bible. In its first verse, the Bible states that, "In the beginning God created the heaven and the earth". If that can be proven to be false, then we have to believe that the rest of the Bible cannot be trusted. I am of the opinion that for this very reason, a lot of effort has been made by godless people to try to disprove the statements of the Bible. I thank God for the many (both saved and unsaved) who have stood up with great argument, to refute those who impose their own ideas as to the beginning of the beginning.

We do not need to believe that God exists to make God exist. Whether we believe it or not, God exists. However these evidences are there for our help, to build up our faith in God. How would we preach Christ if we did not have evidence? Surely it would be much more difficult than it is now.

THE STORY OF EVOLUTION

They say "We began as a natural mineral, we immerged into plant life, and into the animal state; and then into being human, and always we have forgotten our former states, except in early spring when we slightly recall being green again".[18]

How the mineral began, the evolutionists do not explain, but that is not my point. My question rather, is why after all these years don't animals continue to evolve into humans, since there was nothing done to stop the process; and they claim that the universe is so many billions of years old? The process should be repeating itself by now.

In trying to prove their argument that we evolved, they turn to Africa; they say "In Africa there was an animal that stood erect, used tools with care, and began to speak. A new kind of species had appeared, with a brain greater than any before it and a capacity for self-transformation that was new on earth".[19]

---

[18] God and the Evolving Universe. James Redfield; p. 7; Michael Murphy and Sylvia Timbres

[19] God and the Evolving Universe. James Redfield; p. 7; Michael

I will not take time to question the validity of the story, except to ask a few basic questions. Since human being came from an ape like animal, what type of language did the first man speak? Because it seems that he was surrounded by animals alone. To me it seems logical that he should speak like an ape. Remember in that form there was no God to communicate with him.

Darwin's concept says, "Over time, gradual changes continually occur in the physical make-up of plants and animals; genetic mutation and other factors are responsible for these changes. If the changes are great enough and happen over a long period of time, a new species will eventually evolve provided that the plant or animal survives the changes". [20]

This kind of thinking is directly opposite to that which the Bible teaches. The scripture says in **Genesis 2:1, "Thus the heavens and the earth were finished, and all the host of them."**

Everything that was to be created was created

Murphy and Sylvia Timbres; p. 8

[20] Creationism Vs Evolution. Bruno J. Leonce; Green Haven Press Inc. San Diego, California; p. 9

within the six days of creation; there is no such thing as *other life* apart from the life that was created in Genesis chapter one. Everything continues to reproduce after its kind; there is no such thing as evolving from monkey to man; no such thing as life out of no life.

THE GENESIS ACCOUNT

Evolutionists tell us that life came about after millions of years, but what does the account of the Bible say about the creation? As I see it in both accounts, evolution and creation have to be accepted by faith because we were not there; but this does not mean that you don't reason to establish your faith. Evidence helps to establish faith.

The biblical account says that everything was created within six days, by God. And I believe it is a literal six days, not a thousand years as one day, because it is very clearly stated in the Bible.

The Bible made it clear that the evening and the morning is what He is talking about. He was specific; He was talking about day and night as one day – twenty four (24) hour day. So we are sure from the Genesis account that each of the intervals of creation is bounded by evening and morning. So if we believe the biblical account, evolution does not stand because it states that man evolved after millions of years. The Genesis account says that God created man on the sixth day of His creation week, so evolution and the

Bible do not agree as to how we got our earth and living creatures.

The Genesis account states also that the earth did not come from the sun; the earth was created before the sun.

We read in **Genesis 1:9-11, "And God said, Let the waters under the heaven be gathered together unto one place, and let the dry land appear: and it was so. And God called the dry land Earth; and the gathering together of the waters called He Seas: And God saw that it was good. And God said, Let the earth bring forth grass, the herb yielding seed, and the fruit tree yielding fruit after his kind, whose seed is in itself upon the earth: and it was so."**

It was done on the third day of creation. The sun was created on the fourth day; therefore, if the Bible is right, the *big bang theory* falls flat to the ground. The earth did not come from the sun or any other planet. God created it as well as all other planets.

EVOLUTIONISTS

Jonathan D. Sarfati says, "The frame work behind the evolutionist's interpretation, is things made themselves; no divine intervention had happened, and God if he even exists, had not revealed to us knowledge about the past."[21]

So in their research they always seek to look for clues as to how it evolved. It is not objective research; they close the door to the possibility of divine intervention.

In the book entitled "In Six Days," a quotation is made from C.S. Lewis concerning evolution fully. It reads, "If the solar system was brought about by an accidental collision, then the appearance of organic life on this planet was also an accident, and the whole evolution of man was an accident too. If so, then all our thought processes are mere accidents."[22]

He went on to say, "I see no reason for believing

---

[21] In Six Days. John F Ashton; Master Book, pgs. 75-76
[22] In Six Days. John F. Ashton; Master Book; p. 78

that one accident should be able to give a correct account of all other accidents."[23]

If the man and the universe came by accidents, every other thing is an accident. Even if I wanted to believe it, when I look around me, it is just impossible to say it was all an accident.

---

[23] In Six Days. John F. Ashton; Master Book; p. 78

THE GAP THEORY

Almost everybody has his/her own story as to how the world came into being. But the Bible is clear about this very important question, and the Bible gives a very clear answer in the very first book, first chapter and first verse. The answer is unambiguous, "In the beginning God created the heaven and the earth." You either believe the Bible or believe Darwin. The Bible not only says that God created the heaven and the earth; it went on to say how He did it. He spoke them into being. And the Bible gives us the order in which they came.

Now that leads me to a very controversial topic among many theologians and Christians; it is called "The Gap Theory". What is the Gap Theory? It is basically saying that God created the heaven and the earth perfectly. But between Genesis 1:1 and Genesis 1:2 and following, there is a gap. There is a space, there is a time difference. In other words, between Genesis 1:1 and Genesis 1:2 there might have been millions of years.

What the supporters of this theory are saying is

that everything was in order before Satan was cast down to earth; but the moment he was cast down to earth there was chaos; darkness was upon the face of the earth. And so the Spirit of God had to move upon the face of the waters and bring back order on the earth. They used Genesis 1:2 to support their theory. Now this theory will support an earth that may be millions of years old.

But I want to show you how unbiblical this theory is in spite of the fact that many biblical scholars hold on to it. By the way, it is also called the 'Restitution Theory'. Let me say, when God will restore the world it will be once and for all. Righteousness will be rewarded and sin will be punished and Satan and his angels and all those who forget God will be cast into the Lake of Fire (Psalms 9:17 and Revelation 20:12-15).

Now let us go to the heart of the matter. The Bible did not say that when Satan was cast out of heaven there was chaos upon the earth. As a matter of fact the Bible calls the Devil 'the prince of the power of the air' (Ephesians 2:2).

In **Revelation 12:7-12** we have a very interesting

portion of scripture on the future of devil and here is what it says. **"And there was war in heaven: Michael and his angels fought against the dragon; and the dragon fought and his angels, And prevailed not; neither was their place found any more in heaven. And the great dragon was cast out, that old serpent, called the Devil, and Satan, which deceiveth the whole world: he was cast out into the earth, and his angels were cast out with him. And I heard a loud voice saying in heaven, Now is come salvation, and strength, and the kingdom of our God, and the power of his Christ: for the accuser of our brethren is cast down, which accused them before our God day and night. And they overcame him by the blood of the Lamb and by the word of their testimony; and they loved not their lives unto the death. Therefore rejoice, ye heavens, and ye that dwell in them. Woe to the inhabiters of the earth and of the sea! For the devil is come down unto you, having great wrath, because he knoweth that he hath but a short time."**

This prophecy about the devil being cast out of the heavens to the earth is yet future. It has not yet been fulfilled. Furthermore, the heaven that is referred to in that portion of scripture is not the heaven where God's throne is. He was cast out of there by God Himself, not by Michael and his angels. There was no fight; God just cast him out because pride was found in his heart. But he controls the air and of course he roams the earth. But his government seems to be in the air (principalities and powers in heavenly places).

But God gave Adam and Eve to have dominion over the earth. Therefore Satan could not have come and destroyed the earth, before he took the authority from Adam and Eve. So he deceived the woman and took authority from them. Here is what **Luke 4:6** says in regard to that: **"And the devil said to him, All this power will I give thee, and the glory of them: for that is delivered unto me; and to whomsoever I will I give it."** He said it has been given to him. So he could not have destroyed the earth before sin came into the world, and sin came into the world through Adam and Eve (1 Corinthians 15:21-22).

So Satan could not have brought chaos on the

earth before having control over it. He took authority by deceiving Eve. And then death began to reign.

So the truth of the matter is the Bible does not support this Gap Theory, which seems to suggest that there could have been people before Adam and Eve, and also supports the theory that our world could be billions of years old; and that Satan destroyed the first world which God created and God came back and put things together again; to bring back order from chaos. But are they suggesting that the one who caused all this disorder, the devil, was left on earth to cause more chaos? No Sir! Genesis 1:1 tells us without a shadow of a doubt, that God is the creator of the universe; and from verse 2 and following He tells us how God created the universe and how long He took to do that.

Let us examine **Genesis 1:9-10** which is a bone of contention among some. **"And God said, Let the waters under the heaven be gathered together unto one place, and let the dry land appear: and it was so. And God called the dry land Earth; and the gathering together of the waters called he Seas; and God saw that it was good."**

When God created the earth it was under water. The water was covering the earth and God spoke and said let the earth *appear*. This means that the earth was already there. But it could not be seen because it was under the waters. By the way, there was no man to see it; but God wanted to have dry land so He said 'let the dry land appear' and it appeared. And the seas He had to gather together.

Then He commanded the earth to bring forth grass and seed, fruits, and it was so. In other words, God created trees that were already bearing fruits, as well as trees which would bear fruits at a later time. I am trying to say that God created big trees and smaller or younger trees. There were places which were mountainous and there were valleys. God the Master Designer, did it His way!

You see, at times, scientists look at a tree trunk or some stones or some animal bones and they say these things have been around for millions of years; and some times other scientists look at the same material and say that these things are not so old. But that is not the point; the point is God created things that probably looked a million years old, when in fact it was just one day old. When God created Adam, He created an aged man, not a baby. So if you had seen Adam the day after his birth, with our mind set you would probably say that Adam looked a million yeas old, when he was only one day old!

We make furniture and build houses and make them appear more aged than they really are. Why should we find it so hard for God to baffle us with the way He created the universe?

Surely, we don't have all the answers to all the questions that the world is asking. But where we come from and where we are going has been made clear in the Bible. Man can make his own theory and reject the clear teachings of the Bible but for this he will have to answer to the creator of the universe in the other life; and it will be too late to believe the Bible then. Therefore I say to you, believe now and accept the Bible as the Word of God. The theory of evolution was created by man; the world and all that is therein was created by the Master Creator, God.

Noah's Flood Supports Genesis Creation

According to the Bible, there was a worldwide flood that destroyed everything upon the earth, save Noah and what he had in the ark. The account is mentioned by more than one Bible writer; even Jesus Himself mentioned it in the New Testament, but the main account is found in Genesis chapters six through eight.

If the earth was billions of years old like many evolutionists teach, without any flood or major disaster that killed almost all the population, then our earth by now would be over populated with animals and human beings. But if the earth is about seven (7) thousand to ten (10) thousand years old, as a number of Bible scholars believe, and if there was a great flood maybe about two (2) thousand years after creation, we can easily understand why the population of the earth is what it is today. Of course, let us not forget the many more means of birth control available now than in the age before.

I don't want you to miss the point. There are those

who argue that the earth is millions of years old and say there was never a world wide flood which killed all but eight persons who were saved in an ark. Some believe that those persons are right and the Bible is wrong; they prefer to trust men rather than believe in God. If these persons are right, then could you imagine the number of people who would have been on the face of the earth? Where would we have put all those persons?

For instance, if St. Lucia had a million people one million years ago, could you picture what it would be now? The numbers would be staggering. Where would we put people? There would be no space, not even to breathe. The earth, my friend, would have been over-populated a very long time ago. In addition to that the number of births has always out-numbered the number of deaths.

Man is trying his best to deny the record of scripture which is very clear that in the beginning God created the heaven and the earth, and all that is therein.

So the universe came from God. Nothing or no one else could have created it. But man is trying not only to deny the creation of the universe, they are trying to deny that there is a God who has power, far superior to that of human beings. We don't like the idea that one day we will have to stand before God to give an account of how we lived here on earth. But it does not matter what he says; that does not change the fact that there is a living God, the Creator of heaven and earth.

My friends, we just have to look at the universe and immediately we will realize it was not by chance or by a mistake or by accident. A designer had to put it together, and that person is bigger than you and me. This thing is not just created by God; it is sustained by God as well.

Many scientists believe that there was a great flood that covered the face of the whole earth. And some of the fossils that have been found could have been placed in caves and on mountains as a result of the flood. Fossils are no means to support evolution.

Richard Morris says, "Fossils have not always

been interpreted as providing us with evidence about the past evolution of life."[24]

There has been a lot of evidence to support that Noah's flood did take place. There are Babylonian stories about Noah's flood.

Grant R. Jeffery wrote, "I examined the copy of the Babylonian Deluge Tablet displayed in the famous British museum; which holds an enormous collection of archeological discoveries from the Middle East, that supports the truthfulness of many of the scriptural accounts of historical events that occurred more than four millennia ago and contains one of the most important inscriptions from the earliest days of humanity.

The Deluge Tablet is the eleventh book of the Chaldean epic of Gilgamesh (dated 2200 B.C.). The person known as Gilgamesh is Nimrod, the builder of the original city of Babylon, as recorded in Genesis eleven (11). The epic poem, Epic of Gilgamesh, recounts the story of the flood as given to Gilgamesh by an older relative, a man named Nuh-Napishtim (also called Atrahsis) known as the very wise or

---

[24]   The Evolutionists. Richard Morris; p. 14

pious. This Nuh-Napishtim is the Babylonian for Noah. The Babylonian Epic of Gilgamesh contains a remarkable account of the flood."[25]

Now if we can have such records from the Babylonians that have been there for so long, this is telling us something about the biblical accuracy of the flood.

Dr. Ariel A. Roth says, "While evolution proposes that life has been evolving for thousands of millions of years, creation suggests that God created the various forms of life in six days; a few thousand years ago. In the creation model, the Great Flood described as in the Bible, provides the explanation for the fossil layers; while evolution suggests these were formed over eons of time."[26]

So many of the scientists put what date they feel best suits their own findings, and no one can be absolute when it comes to dating fossils; but to me it is much more sensible to see the flood carrying things all into caves and hilltops, than any other means. I am presently reading a book entitled "In Six Days"

---

[25] Unveiling Mysteries of the Bible. Grant R. Jeffery; p. 47
[26] In Six Days. John F. Ashton; p. 95

with fifty scientists who believe in creation and the flood of Noah's day, and I have read many others who are not Christians, but say they believe that there was a world wide flood or there was a time that the sea covered the face of the earth.

There seems to be very strong evidence that there was a flood like what the Bible talks about. If that is true, and the Exodus story is true, why can't we believe that the same man God used to talk about the flood is the same man to whom He revealed how He created the world? Why are we prepared to accept part of Genesis yet reject the beginning of it?

If we believe the scripture according to **2 Peter 1:21, "For the prophecy came not in old time by the will of man: but holy men of God spake as they were moved by the Holy Ghost."** If he was a holy man of God and spoke as he was moved by the Holy Ghost, then all of Genesis is true, and if the beginning is not true, none is true.

My personal opinion about the evolution theory is this: the devil is trying to destroy the very foundation of faith. If God did not create us nor the universe, we are not accountable to Him; and if evolution is right, then the Bible is false. So evolution is one of the craftiest tricks of the devil to make people disbelieve in God.

Many people who are asked whether they believe in Jesus, may say something like this, "I believe there was a man named Jesus who was a true prophet, but not God or the Savior of the world; just a true prophet." Well, if He was a true prophet, this means that what He spoke about in the scriptures are true.

He did speak about the Genesis account, creation, and made it very clear that it was God who created the man. This is the record in **Matthew 19:4, "And He answered and said unto them, Have ye not read, that He which made them at the beginning made them male and female"**.

He was clearly saying that it was God who made man in the beginning, but He was also reminding them that it is written in Genesis; because the same book that talks about the creation of man, talks about the creation of the world also. Now it is left to us as to whom we believe. Will we believe the Bible or some other man? I prefer to believe Jesus than Darwin.

God Creates Out Of Nothing

Man cannot do anything without material; not so with God. Because God is greater than man, He can speak and things begin to happen. God created the universe out of nothing, and if He could not do this, then He is not God. To say that God created the universe without any pre-existent materials whatsoever is what many people cannot understand or refuse to accept. Therefore they try to bring in new theories that they themselves cannot explain; theories that have to be changed from time to time.

We will never understand everything about the creation of the universe, because it was an act of God – it was supernatural. It is just like a miracle; if we can understand everything about a miracle, and explain exactly how it happened, then it is not a miracle. We must accept the fact that we are mortals and because we are mortals, there are things we don't understand; and this is not an easy way out of the discussion, it is fact!! So we should stay with what the Bible says and seek to understand exactly what is written in the Bible and interpret it properly.

Since the world was created supernaturally, and nobody was there when it was created, it means that if we are going to understand it, revelation must come to us by supernatural means. God has to reveal it to us. Well, He has done that in His Word – the Bible. The question right now is, are we willing to accept the Bible as God's revelation to us?

One of the reasons why we are confused about the creation of the universe is because we have not accepted the Bible as the Word of God, and we have not sat down and spent time to see what God says about creation. We have spent all our time trying to understand what Charles Darwin says about how the world came into being, when Darwin did not create the universe!!

The principle applies; if we know the truth well enough, we will be able to identify the false.

The Psalmist says in **Psalm 33:6 – 9, "By the word of the LORD were the heavens made; and all the host of them by the breath of His mouth. He gathereth the water of the sea together as an heap: He layeth up the depth in storehouse. Let all the**

earth fear the LORD: let all the inhabitants of the world stand in awe of Him. For He spake, and it was done; He commanded, and it stood fast."

This talks of the power of God, who is able to create the universe at His word. When God said, "Let there be" there was. As soon as He said it, they came into being; it did not take billions of years to happen, nor did an accident cause it to happen. All it took were His Words.

When Jesus came He demonstrated His supernatural power. To begin with, His birth was supernatural. He was born of a virgin before she knew any man. As he began His earthly ministry, He turned water into wine at His Word. He directed one of His disciples to go to the sea and catch a fish. He said, "The first one you catch, you will find a piece of money in its mouth and that will be sufficient for you to pay your tax," (paraphrased); and it was so. He commanded the raging sea to be still and it immediately obeyed Him. He walked on water. He, supernaturally, in the presence of the multitudes, supplied a large number of loaves and fishes. In the presence of the people, He raised Lazarus from the dead after he had been dead for four days.

All those things were instantaneous. Jesus did them without the help of any medical science or natural ability; it was all by the power of God. He did all that and afterwards they crucified Him; all His blood ran, confirming His death. They put Him in a tomb, sealed the tomb, and set watch over it; yet on the third day He rose from the dead as the Holy Scriptures said He would; and history bears record that He rose from the dead.

Why should one then find it impossible for God to create the heaven and the earth after six days? If I was to argue anything against the creation of the universe, my argument would be this: "Why did God take as many as six days?" He normally does things instantaneously. Maybe the reason for doing it in six days was to teach us a lesson; to teach us that everything does not have to be done the same day, we need to have some rest. Some believe that it is a pattern for us as it was for Israel; to work six days and rest on the seventh.

WE DID NOT COME FROM APES OR BIRDS

The Bible says that man was created in the image of God. No other animal was created in the image of God. We did not come from animals, as evolution teaches. The scripture and science both agree that all flesh is not the same flesh. The human race is unique because he was created uniquely. God did not just speak and he came into being; He took His time and fashioned man; and then breathed His breath into man's nostrils and man became a living soul.

The apostle Paul says in **1 Corinthians 15:39, "All flesh is not the same flesh: but there is one kind of flesh of men, another flesh of beasts, another of fishes, and another of birds."** All flesh is not the same; the human flesh is different from that of birds and beasts. We did not evolve from them. The Bible is abundantly clear that the first man came from the dust of the earth, and was created complete and perfect; and perfection needs no improvement. From the time man sinned, he has not been evolving into a better creature! Man is getting worse day by day; getting to be more sinful.

Genesis 2:7 is very clear when it says, **"And the LORD God formed man of the dust of the ground, and breathed into his nostrils the breath of life; and man became a living soul."**

In **Genesis 3:19** after man had sinned, God said, **"In the sweat of thy face shalt thou eat bread, till thou return unto the ground; for out of it thou was taken: for dust thou art, and unto dust shalt thou return."** Not "..from beast you came and unto beast you shall return" or "..from tree you came and to that you shall return"; but "from dust you came and to it shall you return". Isn't this what happens when we die?

Evolutionists have tried to explain where the problem of pain came from, and have come up with all sorts of theories that do not fit. The Bible is clear; it came as a result of man's sin. Because of man's sin God pronounced curse and pain on him, as well as the ground. We are trying to run away from the idea of God, and we are ending up in confusion. The

Bible is clear on the matter of the origin of life as well as the beginning of sin and sorrow.

EVIDENCE FROM THE FOSSILS

Ray Bohin says, "In the field of paleo-anthropology, the study of human fossils, we must approach the data and interpretation of the scientists involved with a careful and skeptical eye. There are a number of obvious reasons for this healthy skepticism. The most important reason is that they are looking for our evolutionary ancestors. If that is what they are looking for, then that is likely what they will report to have found."[27]

Let me continue making some quotations from this molecular and cell biologist.

"We are now about one hundred and twenty years (120) after Darwin, and knowledge of the fossil record has been greatly expounded. Ironically, we have even fewer examples of evolutionary transition than we had in Darwin's time.

"By this I mean that some of the classic cases of Darwinian change in the fossil record such as, the evolution of the horse in North America, have had

---

[27]   Creation, Evolution, and Modern Science. Ray Bohin; p. 30

to be discarded or modified as a result of more detailed information. There is no simple chronological sequence of horse-like fossils. The story of the gradual reduction from the four-toed horse of sixty (60) million years ago to the one-toed horse of today has been called pure fiction."[28]

Let us continue to unearth the weakness of evolution which Darwin himself was aware of, as well as many of his followers.

Ariel A. Roth, a biologist writes, "If evolution has proceeded over eons of time postulated, we should expect a great number of intermediates between the major types of organisms, but we scarcely find any. Charles Darwin was fully aware of the problem and openly admitted to it in his Origin of Species, stating, *'Why then is not every geological formation and every stratum full of such intermediate links? Geology assuredly does not reveal any such finely graduated organic chain, and this perhaps, is the most obvious and gravest objection that can be urged against my theory.'* Darwin then attributed the problem to the extreme imperfection of the fossil record. We have found

---

[28]   Creation, Evolution, and Modern Science. Ray Bohlin; p. 136

millions of fossils since Darwin's time, and the lack of intermediates remain as a major problem for evolution."[29]

There are many other such things that go against the evolution theory. I would have to make too many quotations, and we would have a book too heavy and embarrassing to carry. But as more light begins to shine, we are seeing more cracks in the evolution theory. Although some of the faithful disciples of this godless religion are trying to plaster the holes, but the foundation is too shaky and more cracks are being formed.

I think it is time an announcement is made from the leading evolutionists, stating that they are wrong, and to ask the world to forgive them and their dead fathers, for trying to prove that God was wrong when He said He created the world in six days. They also need to openly acknowledge that the Bible record is correct concerning the creation of the universe.

---

[29]   In Six Days. John F. Ashton; p. 93

EVOLUTION DENIES GENESIS; JESUS CONFIRMS IT

I prefer to believe the teachings of Jesus than the theory of the evolutionists; especially as we have seen so many problems with that teaching. As I see it, the teachings of Charles Darwin and friends, about how the world began is in great contradiction with God's account in Genesis and the rest of the scripture. I also see the teaching of evolution about the origin of the universe is not just a man seeking to know the truth, but the enemy of mankind – the devil, being the master mind behind all these ideologies, because it is his plan that this teaching defies or seeks to prove that the Biblical account as to how the universe and mankind came about, is not true.

This teaching of evolution has so many unanswered questions and flaws as Darwin himself has acknowledged, and so many great minds have refuted these teachings by showing how these concepts cannot work. Evolution itself cannot explain how life came out of non-life.

Dr. Michael Denton claims, "This subject lends

no support to the theory of evolution. He points out that there is no such thing as a simple cell."[30]

Scientists cannot prove the theory of evolution to be totally true. It is totally against the written Word of God, yet it fills the Universities and Colleges, yes, even the high schools and primary schools of the world. As a matter of fact many of them stopped teaching creation, and replaced it with evolution. One is forced to ask the question "why?"

My answer is this; there is a deliberate attempt to try to deny the God of creation; that does not mean that all who teach it believe it or deny God. But the enemy of God and man, the devil, is so subtle; he will try his best to use whatever means he can to deny that God created the world and all that is in it in six days. So it is to the devil's benefit that this story of evolution stays alive, especially in our schools.

Now it is rather sad to say that this belief is even in our churches today. Because we fail to stand on the infallibility of the Word of God, there is so much compromise with evolution teaching; some of us

---

[30] In Six Days. John F. Ashton; p. 306

have yet to see it as a tool that the devil is using very well to accomplish his purpose.

Let us hear what the Bible says in **Hebrews 1:1-2, "God, who at sundry times and in diverse manners spake in time past unto the fathers by the prophets, hath in these last days spoken unto us by His Son, who He hath appointed heir of all things, by whom also He made the worlds"**.

We have heard what the prophets said concerning creation, especially Moses in the book of Genesis. I think we need to hear what Jesus Christ, the Son of God says in Genesis. He referred to Adam and Eve as real people whom God created male and female, and performed their marriage in the Garden of Eden.

We read it in **Matthew 19:4-5, "And He answered and said unto them, Have you not read, that He which made them at the beginning made them male and female, and said, For this cause shall a man leave father and mother and shall cleave to his wife: and they twain shall be one flesh?"**

He made reference to the children of Adam and Eve as a record in the third chapter of Genesis. In

Matthew 23:24 we read, "That upon you may come all the righteous blood shed upon the earth, from the blood of righteous Abel unto the blood of Zacharias son of Barachias, whom ye slew between the temple and the altar."

Jesus referred to the days of Noah as recorded from the sixth to eighth chapter in Genesis. In **Matthew 24:37 we read, "But as the days of Noah were, so shall also the coming if the Son of Man be.**

And I can give many more quotations where Jesus affirmed the teaching of the book of Genesis, and many of the apostles made reference to the book of Genesis, and to the creation of the universe, and Adam and Eve as a divine act of God.

I prefer to believe Holy men of God and Jesus who was part of the creation process, than men who were just being used as an agent of the devil; and were probably not even so wise as to see that the same devil which beguiled Eve, who they claim really never existed, is beguiling them.

THE THEOLOGICAL IMPORTANCE
OF THE GENESIS CREATION

The account of creation in Genesis is very important theologically. God wanted people to know who He was; not just that He made man, but He created the entire universe. Therefore He has power over the entire universe. Since He is the creator of all things, all have to worship Him and no other. If He can create out of nothing, He has the power to destroy also. So His creation should work in obedience to Him; remembering that all that we have came from Him.

The revelation of creation to Moses and to the children of Israel and to the church is that, the gods of the other nations have no power over the people of God; the gods of the nations are made by man, but the God of Israel and the believers who are in covenant with God, is the creator of heaven and earth. Therefore He has ALL power! There is no god with the power He has. The creator of heaven and earth has power over all heaven and earth.

He created everything out of nothing; this shows

the kind of power that God has. Nobody else could do that.

So the creation of the world had a beginning. The Bible says that God created the entire universe in six days; literal days – morning and evening as one day. So the world is dependant on God because He upholds all things by His power. Just as God brought it forth, He sustains it.

The New Catholic Encyclopedia says, "God not only gives duration to creatures, He intervenes actively in the orientation of the universe. He does not limit himself only to conserving the universe. He also guides it by His providence."[31]

Maybe the best way to conclude this book is to turn our attention to the beloved apostle, Peter, who was dealing with some false teachers of his day.

This is what he says in **2 Peter 2:1, "But there were false prophets also among the people, even as there shall be false teachers among you, who privily shall bring in damnable heresies, even de-**

---

[31] New Catholic Encyclopedia, Second Edition. Berard L. Marthaler; p. 344

nying the Lord that bought them, and bring upon themselves swift destruction."

The Lord bless you, as you continue to thank Him for creating you in His image and likeness.

BIBLIOGRAPHY

Book 1

1. Alister E. Mc. Grath. *The Christian Theology Reader*.

2. Dan Millman and Doug Childers. *Divine Intervention*; Daybreak Books.

3. Deepak Chopra. *To Know God*; Three Rivers Press, New York.

4. Ernest S. Frerichs and Leonard H. Lesko. Exodus, *The Egyptian Evidence*; Winona Lake, Indiana.

5. Grant R. Jeffery. *Unveiling Mysteries Of The Bible*. Frontier Research Publication.

6. Jack Miles. *God, A Biography*; Alfred A. Knopf, New York.

7. James l. Kugel. *The Bible As It Was*; The Belknap Press of Harvard University Press.

8. Jaroslav Pelikan. *The Christian Intellectual*; Harper and Row Publishers, New York.

9. Marianne H. Micks. *Introduction to Theology*. The Seabury Press, New York.

10. Millard J. Erickson. *Christian Theology*; Baker Books.

11. Paul E. Little. *Know Why You Believe*; Intervarsity Press.

12. Richard Elliot Friedman. *The Hidden Face of God*; Harpersan Francisco.

Book 2

1. Amir D. Aczel. *God's Equation*: Four Walls Eight Windows, New York; London.

2. Cornelius G. Hunter. *Darwin's God, Evolution And The Problem of Evil*: Brazos Press.

3. David Wilkinson. *God, Time and Stephen Hawking*: Monarch Books.

4. Ernest J. Sternglass. *Before The Big Bang*: Four Walls Eight Windows, New York.

5. Executive Editor Berard L. Marthaler. *New Catholic Encyclopedia*: Second Edition; For the Catholic University of America Press.

6. Grant R. Jeffery. *Unveiling Mysteries of The Bible*: Frontier Research Publications, Inc.

7. John C. Whitcomb. *The Early Earth*: Revised edition; Baker Book House.

8. John F. Ashton. *In Six Days*: Master Book.

9. John Gribbin. *In The Beginning*: Little, Brow and Company. Boson, New York, Toronto.

10. Lee Smolin. *The Life of The Cosmose*: Oxford University Press.

11. Marcelo Gleiser. *The Dancing Universe*: A. Dulton Book.

12. Paul E. Little. *Know Why You Believe*: Intervarsity Press.

13. Ray Bohlin. *Creation, Evolution, and Modern Science*: Kregel Publications.

14. Stanley J. Grenz. *Theology For the Community of God*: William B. Eerdman's Publishing Company.